THE [ ] OF MCLAREN IN FORMULA 1
to the rhythm of fast lap

Charles Sanz

All rights reserved 2022

Any form of reproduction of this work, in whole or in part, without the express consent of the author, in any graphic, electronic or mechanical medium, including photocopying or recording or any other information storage and retrieval system, is prohibited.

Cover graphic resources: topgear.es / salracing.com / mediotiempo.com / thebestf1.es / motorpasion.com

INTRODUCTION

When Bruce McLaren created his own team to compete in Formula 1, he probably didn't know that he would end up creating one of the most legendary teams in the world's greatest motor racing competition.

In 1966, the Bruce McLaren Motor Racing team made its racing debut, taking its first victory two years later. However, in 1970 an accident took away the magnificent Bruce, and his team faced uncertainty.

Instead of disappearing after the loss of its founder, the McLaren team continued in the competition, achieving its first great triumph thanks to the talent of Brazilian Emerson Fittipaldi.

Aboard a McLaren, James Hunt starred in one of the most spectacular seasons of Formula 1 in his confrontation with Niki Lauda's Ferrari in 1976.

But it was Alain Prost and Ayrton Senna, teammates and at the same time eternal rivals on the track, who led McLaren to become the most powerful team in Formula 1, giving the team the most glorious years of its history.

McLaren was no longer able to dominate as it did between 1988 and 1991, but its goal was always to be at the top of the competition, and drivers like Mika Häkkinen and Lewis Hamilton proved that a McLaren was always to be feared on the track.

Although its recent past is somewhat dark, the history of this great team has shown that McLaren will always have a reserved place among the best teams in Formula 1.

I hope you enjoy its legendary history, in a simple and entertaining way, through these pages.

Bruce McLaren, the origin of a legendary team

Bruce Leslie McLaren was born in Auckland, New Zealand, in the late summer of 1937. At the age of nine, he was diagnosed with Perthes disease, a hip condition that made his right leg longer than his left. Given this handicap, no one would have thought that he would end up becoming one of the legends of Formula 1.

His parents owned a gas station and mechanic shop, so the love of vehicles came early and ran in the family. His father, Les McLaren, was a motorcycle racing enthusiast, but gave it up before his son was born due to injury. After that, he decided to race cars.

Sharing his father's passion, Bruce McLaren made his debut in 1952 at the age of 14 in a mountain race, with an Austin 7 Ulster that his father had prepared for him.

Two years later, he began to compete in official races driving a Ford 10 and an Austin-Healey which led him to compete in F2 with a Cooper-Climax. He stood out for his ability to analyze the car and, thanks to his knowledge after so many years in his father's workshop, he was able to modify and improve it by himself, so that in 1958 he became runner-up in the New Zealand F2 series.

McLaren was selected to participate in the "Driver to Europe" program organized by the New Zealand Grand Prix, with which the organization aimed to export local drivers to the top motor racing competition and surprised with its performance.

At the 1958 Nürburgring Grand Prix, he was able to compete alongside the best drivers in the world, as it was a race that combined F1 and F2 cars, achieving a spectacular fifth place in the final result (behind Tony Brooks, Roy Salvadori, Maurice Trintignant and Wolfgang von Trips), being the best F2 to finish the event.

This display of talent led the Cooper Car Company team to sign him for the 1959 Formula 1 season, alongside Jack Brabham (who had noted Bruce's ability) and Masten Gregroy.

[1]

Bruce made his debut with a fifth place in Monaco, a position he repeated in France, and in his third race in Great Britain he achieved his first podium finishing third. In Germany, Portugal and Italy he had

---
[1] Pinterest.cl

to retire, suffering a terrible second half of his inaugural season in F1, but in the last race at Sebring he redeemed himself by winning the race and achieving his first victory in the top motor racing competition. That year he finished sixth overall.

2

The victory in the United States made him the youngest driver to win a race to date, at the age of 22 years and 104 days.

In 1960 he started in the best possible way by winning in Argentina, and finished on the podium in 5 of the remaining 7 races, which allowed him to be runner-up only behind his teammate Jack Brabham.

1961 was not such a prosperous year for Bruce, who could only reach the podium in Italy, and although he finished in the top six in five of the eight races, he finished 8th overall. In 1962 he was once again

---

[2] Motorsportmagazine.com

victorious at Monaco, and was on the podium four more times, placing him among the best drivers in Formula 1 and finishing third in the season, behind the extraordinary Graham Hill with his BRM and Jim Clark with the Lotus.

In 1963, while continuing to race with Cooper, he set up his own team Bruce McLaren Motor Racing Ltd. In terms of his personal performance, he again had a good season with four podiums, but no wins, which led him to sixth overall. This dynamic was repeated in the following two years with Cooper, although in a slight downward trend. Between 1964 and 1965 he was unable to achieve victory again, although he managed three podiums, repeatedly finishing in the top positions. This led to 7th in 1964 and 9th in 1965.

With this trend that seemed not to improve, in 1966 Bruce McLaren decided to register his own team in Formula 1. Thus, the Bruce McLaren Motor Racing team, which would later become popularly known as McLaren, debuted in the top automobile competition for the first time in its history.

[3] Diariomotor.com

Bruce McLaren and his career in his own team

The single-seater with which Bruce McLaren debuted with his own team, giving rise to the legend of the McLaren team, was the McLaren M2B, a white car with a green stripe in honor of John Frankenheimer's Grand Prix movie (Bruce decided not to use the green color pattern of the British teams, even though he used a British license to participate). It was designed by Robin Herd and in addition to using aluminum for the monocoque, it used mallite (an aeronautical material) to create the chassis.

Throughout his first season he used the Ford 406 3.0 V8 and Serenissima M166 3.0 V8 engine, without really finding power that would allow him to be a champion car.

On his debut in Monaco, Bruce had to retire due to an oil leak when he was in ninth position. This meant that for the second event in Belgium, Bruce opted to swap the Ford engine for the Serenissima. The engine had mechanical problems in the practice session, and Bruce could not even participate in Sunday's race.

Technical problems meant that McLaren did not participate in France, but reappeared in Great Britain to finish sixth. McLaren, as a team, scored its first point in the competition in its first season.

4

However, this sixth position was a slight fleeting triumph, because in the Netherlands the engine blew up again in the practice session,

---

[4] Pinterest.com

which prevented the car from being ready for that test as well as for the following ones in Germany and Italy.

Bruce McLaren returned with his own car in the United States, where he achieved a fifth position, improving his best result and scoring two more points. For the last test in Mexico, an attempt was made to cut the rear end to avoid overheating, but this did not prevent the engine from failing during the race.

McLaren closed its first year with doubts due to reliability problems, but at least the races in which it had not had technical problems, it had managed to finish in points positions, which gave some hope for the future.

For the 1967 season, Bruce McLaren decided to use a new single-seater, the M4B, in the hope that it would be more reliable and more powerful. This time it was powered by the BRM P111 2.1 V8 engine with 280 horsepower (updated version of the engine with which Graham Hill had won the 1962 World Championship).

This car, also designed by Robin Herd, was an improved provisional version of the single-seater from the previous season, while waiting for the definitive M5A. The rear end was shorter than that of its predecessor and incorporated two side fuel tanks so that it could complete a race without refueling.

The McLaren debuted in Monaco in a satisfactory way, where its short wheelbase gave it some advantage and showed to be competitive, and could have achieved a podium but for a pit stop to replace a battery that dropped it to fourth place. At least he managed to score points at the start of the season.

In the second race in Holland, McLaren had an accident that prevented it from finishing the race. Although the M4B was repaired, it caught fire during testing and was eventually retired.

[5]

The M4B was replaced by the M5A, with BRM P142 3.0 engine, this time V12, capable of producing 365 horsepower. It was the first vehicle to use this type of engine.

The new car made its debut in Canada, where despite the rain, McLaren managed to reach fourth position. However, it again had to make a pit stop due to a battery failure, which relegated it to seventh place.

In Italy, Bruce was fighting for fourth place when a broken connecting rod prevented him from finishing the race. In the last two events, he also ended up retiring due to mechanical problems. This completed a season similar to the previous one, where the car was competitive, not to win races, but to finish close to the top positions, at least when there were no breakdowns, more frequent than desirable.

For the 1968 season, Robin Herd enlisted the help of Gordon Copuck to design the McLaren M7A. The M7A incorporated the wings that were being introduced in Formula 1, with the intention of taking

[5] Pinterest.de

advantage of the wind to make the car stick to the ground (inversely to how airplanes use them to take off), getting more grip and speed in the curves.

The engine used in this case was the Ford Cosworth DFV 3.0 V8, of 2933 cc, although in the M7C version it was replaced by an Alfa Romeo engine.

The M7B version changed the central arrangement of the fuel tanks to the sides to improve vehicle control, the M7C changed the cockpit monocoque to a closed model and the M7D incorporated Alfa Romeo's 430 hp T33 3.0 V8 engine, which forced the wheelbase to be increased to 2400 mm.

For the M7, McLaren decided to add a second car to the team, which was driven by New Zealander Denny Hulme. Hulme had made his Formula 1 debut with Jack Brabham's team, with whom he spent three years, becoming world champion in 1967. Therefore, Bruce

---

[6] Ultimatecarpage.com

had a quality teammate with whom he hoped for a prosperous new era for his team.

At the first test of the season in South Africa, the M7A was not yet ready, so only Hulme competed with the M5A from the previous campaign to finish fifth.

In the meantime, the M7A achieved several victories outside the world championship with Bruce winning the Race of Champions and Hulme taking victory in the BRDC International Trophy.

Back in the Formula 1 World Championship, the M7A made its debut in Spain, where McLaren had to withdraw but Hulme managed a fantastic second place that gave the McLaren team its first podium finish.

---

[7] Pinterest.fr

In Monaco, McLaren crashed but Hulme managed to finish fifth. In Belgium, Hulme managed to lead the race but had to retire due to a broken axle. Bruce remained on the track, in second position behind the legendary Jackie Stewart. The Briton had to stop on the last lap for fuel, which allowed Bruce to take his first victory with his own team, even though he thought he had crossed the finish line in second place because he did not expect Stewart to stop for fuel with one lap to go.

[8] Pinterest.com

Bruce McLaren became only the second driver, after Jack Brabham, to win a Formula 1 race with his own team.

However, after the team's first win, they began to suffer a decline in performance, mainly due to Goodyear tire degradation, with Hulme struggling to score points and Bruce out of the points.

It was five races later, in Italy, after the removal of the wings and the arrival of new Goodyear tires, that the McLaren team began to improve again.

In Italy, the increase in performance was spectacular. Although Bruce had to retire due to an oil leak, Hulme managed to win the race, giving the team its second ever victory.

This meant that for the last three races of the season, McLaren added a third car to the team, to be driven by Dan Gurney. The American had debuted with Ferrari in Formula 1, achieving in 1959 two podiums and a fourth place in the four races in which he participated with the Italian team.

After that he had a fateful season in Owen Racing Organisation where he could only finish one of the seven races in which he participated, finishing tenth. After that he drove two years for Porsche with better results, achieving a victory and four podiums. He continued to be successful for three years in the Brabham structure, with two more victories and eight podiums, after which he moved to the Anglo American Racers team.

Because Anglo had run out of funds to continue its Formula 1 program, Gurney eventually became a McLaren driver.

Gurney did not have a great debut, having to retire due to overheating in Canada, but Hulme and Bruce continued the team's good run, achieving an incredible double, with Denny taking the victory.

In the United States, Denny Hulme had mathematical options to become world champion, but a spin that damaged the car, resulting in a broken gearbox that finally caused an accident, ended his chance to be champion, while Gurney finished fourth and Bruce sixth.

In the last race in Mexico, Hulme still had a chance to be champion, but the breakage of a shock absorber again caused an accident, ending all his chances of winning the championship, which went to Graham Hill. Bruce finished second in Mexico to end a very satisfactory year, where Hulme could have been champion, but at least the first victory in the history of the team was achieved in a car capable of fighting for victories.

McLaren achieved an extraordinary runner-up in the constructors' championship, 13 points behind the Lotus driven by legends such as Graham Hill and Jim Clark.

In the 1969 season, Bruce McLaren kept Denny Hulme as teammate, with Gurney out of competition this year.

[9] en.wikipedia.org

The M7 continued to be used while waiting to develop the M9A, the new version with four-wheel drive. This single-seater was not successful, and was only driven in Great Britain by the British driver Derek Bell, with whom he eventually retired. Therefore, the M7 was again the official team car for this season.

Wings were again the protagonist this season, with no clear choice of the best option to use them. Versions with rear wings mounted on the suspension and front wings were tested during some practices, without finding a convincing configuration. Over-suspension wings were first banned and then allowed again. Finally, McLaren opted for a tray-shaped rear wing.

The M7 got off to an optimistic start with a podium finish for Hulme and fifth place for Bruce in South Africa. In the second race in Spain, it was Bruce who took second place and Hulme fourth. However, despite the recurring podium finishes (Bruce took three for the season and Denny one), it was clear that they did not have the ability to compete for victories as they had the previous year.

In fact, the team only achieved a single victory during 1969, and for that it was necessary to wait until the last race of the year, where Hulme managed to win the race in Mexico.

[10] Deviantart.com

Bruce, who had been fifth in the previous season, improved to third in the final standings. On the other hand, Hulme, who had been 3rd and had even had several chances to become world champion, dropped to 6th.

As a team, McLaren dropped to fourth place behind Matra, Brabham and Lotus, so the dream of a constructors' title after the 1968 runner-up finish seemed to be slipping away.

In 1970, Bruce McLaren and Denny Hulme were again the team's drivers, in a team that would change throughout the year.

The single-seater used in this season was the M14A, which was actually a slight evolution of the M7, where the most important change was the use of internal rear brakes instead of external ones. The engine continued to be the Ford Cosworth DFV V8, although a version called M14D would end up using the Alfa Romeo T33.

---

[11] Carpixel.net

The 1970 season began with ups and downs, with Denny Hulme achieving a podium in the first race and Bruce in the second, but with frequent mechanical problems that caused them to retire alternately in the first three races.

After these first three races, misfortune would mark the future of the McLaren team forever.

During a Can-Am car event at Goodwood on June 2, 1970, Bruce McLaren suffered a fatal accident testing the McLaren M8D that resulted in his death and the loss of one of the greatest drivers in history.

In addition to his Formula 1 career, McLaren cars had dominated the Can-Am series in 1967, 1968 and 1969 (the latter year winning every race), and he won the 1966 24 Hours of Le Mans in a Ford GT40 alongside Chris Amon.

The death of Bruce McLaren, founder of the McLaren team, left the team in a complicated situation with an uncertain future.

[12] News.cars.com

The McLaren team after the death of founder Bruce McLaren

In addition to the death of Bruce McLaren, after the Monaco Grand Prix, Denny Hulme was also unable to continue the championship after suffering an accident during practice for the Indianapolis 500.

This left the team without its founder and two drivers, making it impossible for McLaren to participate in the Belgian race.

Faced with such an uncertain situation, Teddy Mayer, who had worked with Bruce in the formation of the team since 1962 and was also the largest shareholder, took control of McLaren.

For the fifth round in the Netherlands, he managed to bring together three drivers so that three McLaren single-seaters could continue their history beyond their founder.

13

One of these three drivers was already known to the team, American Dan Gurney, who drove the M14A for the next three races.

The second of them was Peter Gethin. The Briton in 1969 had been champion of the Formula 5000 European Championship (he would also win it in 1970), and with this McLaren opportunity he made his debut in Formula 1.

---

[13] Pinterest.nz

The third car was driven by Andrea de Adamich, who used a version of the old M7 with an Alfa Romeo engine. The Italian had made his Formula 1 debut in 1968 in South Africa, the first round of the championship, with Ferrari, and had beaten his teammates Chris Amon and Jacky Ickx in the qualifying session.

However, he had to retire in the race, and a subsequent accident in the Race of Champions left him unable to participate for the rest of the season.

In 1969, the Ferrari crisis made Adamich decide to compete in endurance racing, but in 1970, together with McLaren, he again had the opportunity to participate in Formula 1.

---

[14] en.wikipedia.org

McLaren therefore had an old acquaintance and two inexperienced drivers to continue its Formula 1 history. Both Gurney and Gethin had to retire during the race, while Andrea de Adamich did not even qualify to participate.

For the next race in France, Denny Hulme returned to bring some experience and hope to the team, and achieved a creditable fourth position, also Gurney got a good sixth position, while Andrea was again unable to qualify.

In the seventh race in Great Britain, Hulme, Gurney and Adamich were the McLaren representatives, and while Gurney retired again and Adamich was still unable to qualify, Denny Hulme at least managed a podium that allowed the team to stay afloat and not fall into an irreversible trend.

---

[15] F1.fandom.com

16

For the eighth race, Gethin replaced Gurney, although his fate was the same, another retirement, while Hulme continued to save the team with a new podium.

The same line-up was repeated in Austria, this time with Hulme dropping out. Gurney was at least able to finish in tenth position and Andrea finally managed to qualify for a race and finish it, in 12th place.

For the tenth race in Italy there were four members of the Bruce McLaren Motor Racing team on track, with the M14D (now powered by Alfa Romeo) of the Italian Nanni Galli, in his only participation with the team after failing to qualify.

Hulme was fourth at Monza, with Andrea de Adamich improving to eighth, this time Gethin failing to qualify for the race.

In the last three races of the season, Hulme, Gethin and Andrea de Adamich continued to be the regular drivers in a squad that had varied greatly throughout the season, with Hulme taking another

---

[16] Motorsportimages.com

podium finish in Mexico as his best result and Gethin scoring in Canada.

Thus ended a turbulent year in which the team had to overcome the loss of its founder, with Denny Hulme's four podiums that allowed the New Zealander to be fourth in the final standings and McLaren to occupy fifth place in the list of constructors, equaling Brabham in points, behind Lotus, Ferrari and March.

In 1971, the goal was to regain stability so that the team could once again aspire to win races. At the team level, it was decided to keep only two drivers: Denny Hulme and Peter Gethin.

As for the single-seater, the development of the new M19A fell to Ralph Bellamy, as Gordon Copuck was busy designing the single-seater for the Indianapolis 500.

The M19A was nicknamed the crocodile car because of its appearance, as two of the three gas tanks were incorporated into the sides giving it the appearance of this animal.

Innovative internal coil-over shock absorbers were incorporated to improve the stability of the single-seater, but were eventually replaced by more traditional systems as they did not achieve the expected results.

Throughout the season, the Ford Cosworth DFV engine was used, abandoning the Alfa Romeo engine.

---

[17] Pinterest.com

The season got off to an encouraging start, at least for Denny Hulme, who managed to finish sixth, fifth and fourth in the first three races, while Gethin suffered two retirements.

However, as the season progressed, reliability problems became more frequent and withdrawals more recurrent.

After the seventh race, Gethin left the team after signing for Yardley Team BRM, and was replaced by Jackie Oliver. The Briton participated in 1967 with a Formula 2 in the German race, finishing fifth, which made Team Lotus sign him for the 1968 season, where he got a podium in Mexico.

In 1969 he raced with the Owen Rasing Organisation, retiring in eight of the ten races in which he competed, and in 1970 he raced with Yardley Team BRM, retiring in nine of the 12 races of the season and failing to qualify in one of them.

[18]

---

[18] F1forgottendrivers.com

Oliver managed a ninth place in Austria and seventh place in Italy, while Hulme continued to suffer one retirement after another, only managing a fourth place in Canada as the most remarkable result, to finish 13th in the drivers' standings.

This season, in which the lack of reliability was so much in evidence, the McLaren team dropped to sixth place with only 10 points, and began to move away from success.

Yardley Team McLaren, between failure and revival

In 1972, the team was renamed Yardley Team McLaren... and it was really the most significant change, as the car that continued to be used was the M19, with some changes trying to improve its reliability and performance by creating the M19C version.

Denny Hulme continued to be the main driver and the hope of the British team, while his main teammate this season was Peter Revson. The American had participated in Formula 1 in 1964, splitting it between his own team and Reg Parnell Racing without scoring points. In 1971 he had only participated in the North American race with Elf Team Tyrrell, retiring.

However, in 1971 he had managed to become Can-Am champion ahead of Denny Hulme, so McLaren incorporated again a driver with little experience in Formula 1, but successful in other types of races.

The campaign started much more optimistically than the previous one. Denny Hulme made the changes to the M19 profitable and after finishing second in Argentina, he was finally able to achieve a great victory for the team in the second race in South Africa. Meanwhile, Revson also achieved very good results, adding to the podium in South Africa.

This promising start led to the addition of a third McLaren for the fourth race, driven by Brian Redman, who had driven occasionally in Formula 1 for Lola Cars, Cooper Car Company, Frank Williams Racing Car and Team Surtees, achieving a podium finish in Spain in 1968.

The middle part of the championship was not as prolific as the beginning and lowered a little the euphoria, but McLaren was able to recover to be again among the top positions in the last third of the championship.

Although another victory was not achieved again, Hulme managed to get on the podium five more times and Revson also finished in the

---

[19] Hemmings.com

top three on four occasions. Meanwhile, Brian Redman managed to finish in the top ten in all three races in which he participated with McLaren.

With these good results, Denny Hulme finished third in the championship, returning again to the top, only surpassed by the champion Emerson Fittipaldi and Jackie Stewart. Peter Revson managed to be fifth, which in team returned McLaren to the third position of constructors, only behind Lotus and only 4 points behind Tyrrell.

McLaren was once again among the greats, still without being a clear candidate for the title, but with hope for the future.

In the last race of the year in the United States, McLaren had included in its line-up the South African Jody Scheckter, who was making his debut in the competition after his success in Formula 3.

In 1973, the enthusiasm for the latest results was joined by the return of Gordon Coppuck to participate in the development of the new M23, with the help of John Barnard. Improvements that had been developed on the McLaren M16 at Indianapolis were incorporated into the M19, and the Ford Cosworth engine continued to be used.

[20]

---

[20] en.m.wikipedia.org

Denny Hulme was once again McLaren's main standard bearer, continuing in the company of Peter Revson, who was joined by Jody Scheckter with an expanded program after making his debut in the last race of the previous season.

The M23 did not arrive in time for the start of the season, so the first two races were run with the previous year's M19, with Denny Hulme taking the podium in Brazil.

In the debut of the M23 in South Africa, Denny Hulme made his debut with pole position, although in the race he finally finished fifth.

Good results were slow in coming, with Hulme and Revson finishing in the top ten, but unable to repeat a podium finish in the first third of the championship. However, everything changed in Sweden, where Denny Hulme again took yet another victory for McLaren.

The question then was to see if the M23 was a car capable of fighting for victories constantly, or only had the potential to achieve some

---

[21] Src.es

occasional triumph. The answer came two races later, when Peter Revson won in Great Britain. In addition to this new victory, the American also won in Canada.

In addition to the wins, Revson managed to finish in the top five in five of the last seven races, although Hulme had an uncertain end to the season, finishing lower than tenth on numerous occasions. Both drivers placed fifth and sixth in the championship respectively. Scheckter retired on four occasions, finishing ninth in the only race he did not retire.

These results allowed McLaren to finish third in the constructors' championship, although far behind Lotus and Tyrrell in points. This was in line with the general feeling: a car capable of winning races had been achieved, but more consistency and authority was needed to make them more frequent and to aspire to a world championship at last.

The arrival of Emerson Fittipaldi and the first championship

By the 1974 season, McLaren had proven it had a car capable of winning races. All it needed was a driver who could get the most out of it. And for that, it signed Brazilian Emerson Fittipaldi.

Fittipaldi, who had become champion in 1972 in his third year with Lotus and in Formula 1, had been runner-up in 1973 in his particular battle with Jackie Stewart.

McLaren relied on his talent to make that leap in quality that had always been missing to achieve a constructors' championship.

Along with Denny Hulme as the team's main drivers, they were also joined by British driver Mike Hailwood to start the campaign.

After his successful participation in motorcycling (top class champion in 1962, 1963, 1964 and 1965), Hailwood had also raced with Reg Parnell Racing in Formula 1 between 1963 and 1965, although only the second year with a full program, before participating in two races with Team Surtees in 1971 and enjoying two full programs in 1972 and 1973, where he achieved his first and only podium.

The single-seater this season continued to be the M23, although Fittipaldi helped to incorporate the knowledge acquired during his time at Lotus.

In this way, the good results did not take long to come. Denny Hulme gave McLaren the victory in the season opener in Argentina.

---

[22] F1-fansite.com

However, the New Zealander failed to repeat his victory and the season was left in the hands of the talented Brazilian driver, who became the team's star. Fittipaldi won the second race of the year, on home soil, and repeated his triumph three races later.

However, once again a promising start seemed to stall, as McLaren failed to win a race for the next eight races.

After the eleventh race, Hailwood left the team after a podium finish in South Africa and repeated top ten finishes.

Those who joined the team were the British David Hobbs and the German Jochen Mass. Hobbs had experience in the famous Le Mans race (he had been champion in 1962) and had participated in sporadic races in Formula 1 with an eighth position as best result with a BRM in Great Britain in 1967. This season he only participated in two races with McLaren, finishing seventh and ninth.

As for Jochen Mass, European Touring Car Championship champion, he participated in 3 races with Team Surtess in 1973, with whom he also repeated with a broader program in 1974, only being able to finish two races out of the 11 he entered. That meant that this season he participated with McLaren in the last two races of the year, finishing 16th in Canada and 7th in the United States.

In the meantime, and despite the fact that the team seemed to have stagnated throughout the year in 1974 with Fittipaldi's second victory in the fifth race, the Brazilian had managed to stay consistently in the top positions, so that in a year in which no one was winning hegemonically, he had a chance of becoming champion in the final stretch of the season.

His main rival for the title was Clay Regazzoni driving for Ferrari. With two races to go, Fittipaldi returned to victory by winning the Canadian race, while the Swiss was second. This meant that both drivers were equal on points at the last and exciting race in the United States (although Scheckter with his Tyrrell also had options).

In a race that saw the fatal accident of Helmuth Koinigg, a problem with the front shock absorber complicated the race for Clay

Regazzoni. Fittipaldi took advantage to finish in fourth position, enough to win a new world championship for him, and the first for McLaren as a constructor.

23

Denny Hulme finished seventh in qualifying, ending his career in Formula 1, having become one of the most outstanding drivers in the early years of the McLaren team.

In 1975, the Marlboro Team McLaren (a name it had already acquired during the previous season), the team retained Emerson Fittipaldi, with whom it hoped to have begun a new era of success.

---

[23] Topgear.com

His teammate and the only McLaren driver besides the Brazilian this season was German Jochen Mass, who had already participated in the last two races the previous season.

The car was once again the M23 with evolutions such as a new 6-speed gearbox and aerodynamic reinforcements at the rear and different rear ends that were changed several times giving rise to different chassis throughout the year.

With Fittipaldi at the helm, 1975 started brilliantly, with the Brazilian winning the inaugural race in Argentina and taking second place in Brazil, where Jochen Mass also stood on the podium. The German also took victory in Spain, the fourth race of the year.

[24] F1-fansite.com

However, as in previous years, the wins seemed to stop after a profitable start, and the next victory took six races to come, when Fittipaldi took first place in Germany. It was also the third and last of the year for McLaren.

Despite this, Emerson Fittipaldi once again proved to be a driver with great consistency, adding four podiums to his two victories, which allowed him to be at the top of the standings.

However, he did not count on a talented Niki Lauda who, in his second year at Ferrari, achieved 5 victories and proved to be unbeatable, relegating Fittipaldi to the drivers' runner-up position.

Jochen Mass, who added three podium finishes to his victory, could only finish sixth, which meant that McLaren finished third, just one

---

[25] Deviantart.com

point behind in its battle with Brabham, although far behind the champion Ferrari.

The euphoria achieved with the previous year's championship was diminished, but there was still confidence in returning to the top.

The battle between James Hunt and Niki Lauda

At the end of 1975, Fittipaldi announced his departure to his brother Copersucar Fittipaldi's team, which left McLaren without its star, and without the possibility of signing one of the protagonists of the competition since they were all under contract with their respective teams.

To accompany Jochen Mass, the McLaren team opted to sign James Hunt. The Briton had participated three seasons in Formula 1 with the Hesketh Racing team, achieving eight podiums and even a victory in the Netherlands the previous season, good results considering that he was participating with a team that was not one of the most prominent.

Again with the M23 evolved to the M23D version, the controversial James Hunt, characterized by his rebellious "bad boy" attitude, started in the shadow of Niki Lauda's Ferrari. While the Austrian came first or second in the first six races, Hunt managed to come second in South Africa and win the race in Spain, retiring in the remaining four.

His victory in Spain was also annulled, as the McLaren was wider than what was established by the regulations, although later the victory was returned to him as 1.5 centimeters was not enough to breach the regulations.

Niki Lauda's lead was such that at the halfway point of the championship he was 30 points ahead of James, but the brutal accident that almost cost the Austrian his life in Germany meant that Lauda was unable to participate in the next two races.

James Hunt took advantage by adding five more victories to the one in Spain in the second half of the championship. Despite this, at the final round in Japan, he was still three points behind Niki Lauda, who had made a heroic comeback to the competition and was still scoring points despite the pain of injuries.

---

[26] F1aldia.com

With rain flooding the track under Mount Fuji, Niki Lauda (as well as other drivers) decided to be cautious and withdraw from the race, while Hunt, more risky, decided to participate in search of his first world championship.

James needed to be fourth, but a tire problem caused him to pit late in the race, dropping him to fifth. However, in the final laps of the event, he managed to overtake two positions and win the world championship in an unexpected way.

McLaren won the drivers' championship, but could not beat Ferrari in the constructors' championship. Jochen Mass could only manage two podiums throughout the season, finishing ninth in the final standings, while Clay Regazzoni, fifth, achieved a victory and three podiums that gave Ferrari the victory over McLaren.

---

[27] Semana.com

In 1977, Marlboro Team McLaren continued to count on Hunt and Mass as drivers, seeking this time not only to win the drivers' championship, but also the constructors' championship.

To this end, Coppuck developed the M26... which proved problematic in testing with overheating problems. This forced a revision of the radiator, so the season started with the M23 from the previous season. The delay in its optimization was such that the M26 was not ready until near the end of the 1977 season.

With the previous year's car, Hunt and Mass tried to fight back, but it was evident that McLaren did not have the ability to fight for victories.

Although they managed to be among the first positions, McLaren was far behind Lauda and Reutemann's Ferrari, but also behind Andretti's Lotus and even Scheckter's Wolf. With the entry of the M26, the dynamic of results changed.

[28]

Although the first results were not convincing and Hunt came to detest the car, efforts to improve its performance and reliability were

---

[28] Motorpasion.com

noticeable throughout the season. In the second half of the championship, the Briton managed to achieve three victories... although he had to retire in five of the last seven races (in two of them, Austria and Canada, when he was leading the race). This showed that the M26 was a powerful but fragile car.

In the end, James Hunt finished fifth in the final standings, with teammate Jochen Mass sixth behind him, 15 points behind.

The improvement in the second half of the championship allowed McLaren to finish third, only two points behind Lotus, although far behind a hegemonic Ferrari driven by Lauda. However, there was hope of fighting for the title again if the reliability of the M26 was improved.

This season, Canadian Gilles Villeneuve made his Formula 1 debut with McLaren in the British race, finishing 11th. Italian Bruno Giacomielli also drove in a race for McLaren, but eventually retired on home soil.

In 1978, James Hunt continued to be the team's main driver, but this time his teammate was Patrick Tambay, who replaced Jochen Mass.

The Frenchman had made his Formula 1 debut the previous year, participating in the second half of the season with Theodore Racing Hong Kong, achieving creditable fifth places.

---

[29] Minicar.es

Despite a promising start with Hunt and Tambay scoring points in Argentina in 1978, both drivers had to retire in the next two races, and James accumulated three more consecutive retirements with an M26 that did not improve in reliability.

In addition to this problem, the powerful Lotus 79 implemented the ground effect that gave it an overwhelming advantage over the other single-seaters. With the new ground effect that "glued" the cars to the asphalt and allowed a higher cornering speed, the M26 soon became outdated.

Halfway through the season, the M26's pontoons were enlarged and smaller front and rear wings were used to try to take advantage of the ground effect, but the results were not as expected and the team continued to sink, with James Hunt finishing 13th with only 8 points, the same as his teammate Tambay, which led to his retirement from the McLaren team at the end of the season.

Italian Bruno Giacomelli replaced Tambay in five races, but did not score in any of them.

McLaren dropped to eighth place in the constructors' world championship, and suffered a hard blow to its trajectory.

[30]

---

[30] Flickr.com

Uncertainty at McLaren and the "shitty box".

In 1978, Marlboro Team McLaren needed to renew itself if it wanted to remain among the best teams in Formula 1. To this end, the M28 had been developed with the help of the wind tunnel to implement the ground effect that had turned the Lotus into an invincible single-seater.

The result was a larger and bulkier vehicle, which affected its top speed, making it one of the slowest in speed tests. In addition, the ground effect did not work as expected and it did not get a good grip.

A large car had been chosen to have a wider bottom to take advantage of the ground effect, but such a large front end ended up destabilizing the single-seater.

This forced a redesign of the chassis throughout the year, creating a total of three variations of the M28.

31

After the announcement of James Hunt's departure, McLaren thought of the Swede Ronnie Peterson as his replacement, but his fatal accident in Italy at the end of 1978 prevented the signing from taking place.

Instead, McLaren opted for John Watson to join Tambay for the 1979 season. The Briton had finished sixth in the previous campaign with Parmalat Racing Team, on an upward trajectory in his six years in Formula 1 where he had achieved 6 podiums.

---

[31] Commons.wikimedia.org

Watson made his McLaren debut with a podium in Argentina, but it was the only one he achieved in the first half of the championship, openly showing his dissatisfaction with a car he described as a "shit box".

Although Watson managed to score on two more occasions, Tambay finished tenth or worse in the races he managed to finish, so the car was scrapped and the M29 was used from the ninth race onwards.

The M29 did not improve the results much either, and although Watson managed to score in 4 of the remaining 7 races, he never again reached the podium, finishing with 15 points in ninth place in the championship, with Tambay unable to score any points.

This placed the team in seventh position in the constructors' championship and prolonged its bad streak.

In 1980, the pressure on the team and the need for good results was already evident.

---

[32] Elsofadelaf1.blogspot.com

Patrick Tambay left the team and a rookie Alain Prost, who had been French Formula 3 champion in 1978 and 1979 and European Formula 3 champion in 1979, was signed to accompany Watson.

[33]

However, the performance of the M29 was similar to the previous season, if not worse. Struggling to finish in the top ten, Watson only managed to score points in the United States, finishing fourth, while Prost, despite scoring points in the first two opening races, failed to score again in the next five races.

This accelerated the development of the M30 in an attempt to halt the team's downward trajectory. It was a version of the M29 that tried to enhance the ground effect, and was driven only by Alain Prost in the last four races of the championship. Although he finished sixth in the first and seventh in the second, he had to retire in Canada and did not qualify for the United States, so the M30 was abandoned.

---

[33] Motorsportmagazine.com

At the end of the season, John Watson was 11th with 6 points, while Alain Prost finished 16th with 5 points. These 11 points placed McLaren in ninth position in the constructors' championship, and it seemed that the team was unable to improve, even fearing for its continuity.

The arrival of Ron Dennis

In 1980, McLaren's main sponsor Philip Morris began pressuring the team to seek a visible improvement, which led to a merger with Ron Dennis' Project Four Formula Two team, which shared a sponsor. Following the merger, the team moved from Colnbrook to the new base in Woking, and although Dennis and Mayer shared management, Mayer eventually departed, leaving Dennis as leader.

This change brought the designer John Barnard to the team, who intended to design an innovative carbon fiber chassis, instead of using the usual aluminum. With the money obtained after the merger, he was finally able to materialize his idea and the MP4/1 became the first single-seater to use carbon fiber, something that would be incorporated in Formula 1 until it became essential.

This new material made it possible to create a single-seater with much less weight, and therefore faster, without compromising its strength.

Thus, a new era began at McLaren and, after the departure of Alain Prost to Renault, Andrea de Cesaris joined the team as a driver to accompany John Watson.

The Italian had made his debut in the final part of the 1980 championship, participating in two races with Alfa Romeo. In the first one, his engine failed after eight laps and in the second one he suffered an accident on the second lap.

Therefore, Watson once again found himself with a driver without much Formula 1 experience as a teammate.

The start of the season was somewhat uncertain, with Watson finishing higher than tenth, but failing to score in the first six races. However, in Spain Watson achieved third place and a podium finish that rekindled the team's hopes. This hope was further magnified with second place in France, and victory in Spain in three consecutive races that revived the team.

[35]

---

[35] Eventosmotor.com

The rest of the season saw the euphoria subside, although Watson scored another podium finish in Canada with second place and added points in Germany and Austria.

On the other hand, Andrea de Cesaris did not match his teammate's performance, scoring only one point in San Marino. This meant that McLaren only scored 28 points, finishing in sixth position, but at least the results of previous years were improved and they had even managed to achieve a new victory.

In 1982, McLaren announced the signing of Niki Lauda, who was returning to Formula 1 after retiring in 1979. Although the ground effect had changed the way of driving since then, Watson finally had an experienced partner who, together with the new improvements of the MP1/4 could complete the McLaren revival.

Thus, the start of 1982 was encouraging. Lauda finished fourth in the opening race in South Africa and Watson sixth, but the Briton managed to get on the podium in the following race.

The Austrian won the third race in the United States. Watson also returned to victory in the fifth race, Belgium, and repeated his triumph two races later.

All these victories brought McLaren back to the top of the competition, and even to dream of a new championship... although the second half of the season the results were more moderate. Only Niki Lauda scored a new victory again, in Great Britain, and both drivers only climbed back onto the podium once more each.

Despite this, McLaren was competing for both the drivers' and constructors' titles until the end. John Watson fought for the championship with Keke Rosberg's Williams and both arrived with options to the last race in Las Vegas (third race in the United States that year). Watson needed to win the race and that Rosberg did not score, something complicated and that did not materialize as the fifth place gave the title to the Finnish Williams driver. But at least McLaren felt again what it was like to fight to win a world championship until the end.

In the constructors' world championship something similar happened, McLaren had options until the end, but finally it was Ferrari who managed to win the championship, making McLaren the runner-up by only 5 points of difference.

At last, it seemed that McLaren was back and could fight for new championships.

In the early 1980s, the turbocharged engines introduced by Renault were beginning to establish themselves in other teams as a replacement for the classic naturally aspirated engines and were beginning to make their mark in the competition. If McLaren wanted to continue its rise and stay on top, it had to adapt to them.

For this adaptation, Ron Dennis partnered with sponsor Techniques d'Avant Garde (TAG) to acquire turbocharged engines manufactured by Porsche.

The season started with Cosworth engines, but they were eventually replaced by TAG TTE PO1 1.5 L V6t engines for the E version of the MP4/1.

John Watson and Niki Lauda continued as team drivers, hoping that the switch to the turbo engine would not adversely affect them.

The 1983 period with the Ford engine was a slight step backwards, although John Watson won the second race in the United States West (starting from the back of the grid), with Niki Lauda taking the podium in the first two events of the year. From then on, reliability problems became noticeable and when the races were finished, it was difficult to score points. Watson returned to the podium on two more occasions, while Niki Lauda failed to finish in the top three again during the season.

McLaren returned to the top, but lost the ability to fight for the championship. With this scenario, the transition to the TAG engine was made... disastrously. In 3 of the 4 races in which it was used, both cars ended up retiring. In the last one, Lauda managed to finish, but he did so in eleventh position.

John Watson finished sixth with 22 points and Niki Lauda finished tenth with 12 points. Overall, McLaren dropped to fifth place, another hard blow in a year in which they wanted to be fighting for the world championship again.

The return and glory of Alain Prost at McLaren

In 1984, Alain Prost returned to McLaren after his disagreement with Renault. The Frenchman had been runner-up the previous season, and publicly showed his anger with his team, with a car whose reliability problems had prevented him from winning the championship.

John Watson left the team when his request for a salary increase was not accepted (he wanted to receive more money than Niki Lauda), and with Prost joining Niki Lauda, McLaren got a very capable driver line-up.

For them, the MP4/2 was developed, with chassis designed by Steve Nichols, John Barnard, Alan Jenkins, Gordon Kimball, Bob Bell and Tim Wright, this year already powered throughout the campaign by the TAG Porsche engine with 650 horsepower for racing and capable of squeezing out 800 horsepower for qualifying with the turbo at full throttle.

Another advantageous feature of the MP4/2 was that it used carbon fiber brakes, which provided more braking efficiency, except on street circuits.

The new McLaren was very effective from the start, with Alain Prost winning the first race in Brazil and Niki Lauda the second in South Africa.

---

[36] Snaplap.net

Both drivers proved invaluable during the development of the car, providing significant input and feedback, so this success was sustained throughout the year.

With an efficient car and two of the best drivers on the grid in the squad, McLaren not only managed to fight for a championship again, but achieved absolute dominance throughout the season.

The team won twelve out of the sixteen races, achieving four double wins. McLaren not only achieved the triumph, but also became the clear dominator of Formula 1.

Unchallenged, the drivers' championship was contested by the two McLaren drivers, who arrived at the final round in Portugal with a chance of becoming champions. Alain Prost won the Portuguese race, but Niki Lauda took advantage of his slight advantage in points and, finishing second, won his third world championship, with the added merit of achieving it after having retired and returned to competition.

[37]

---

[37] Maxf1.net

McLaren's overwhelming dominance saw it almost triple the points total of the second-placed manufacturer, Ferrari, allowing McLaren to win its second constructors' title in history.

McLaren thus returned to the top of Formula 1, and the challenge remained to see if this time it could maintain its success over time.

Thus, in 1985, the team and single-seater were repeated (with slight modifications), in the hope of achieving a new championship.

The new season began with Alain Prost winning in Brazil, which augured a new year of dominance, and continued throughout the year showing a great performance, with four more victories and six additional podiums, finishing no further than fourth place in the races in which he did not have to retire due to a technical problem.

Niki Lauda's performance was not so good, having to retire seven times in the first eight races, thus conditioning his season. In the second part of the season he achieved a victory in Holland, but an accident in Belgium made him miss two races, and when he returned it was only to accumulate two more retirements. This caused him to drop to tenth position in the drivers' world championship.

With Niki Lauda out of the fight, Prost's main rival for the championship was the Italian Michele Alboreto with Ferrari, but he was not a really dangerous opponent and finally managed to lead him by 20 points in the final standings. Alain Prost thus won the world championship he had been denied at Renault.

Niki Lauda's difficult season meant that McLaren had to fight with Ferrari for the constructors' title, but Alboreto's teammate in the Italian team, the Swede Stefan Johansson, did not score any victories and finally Prost's performances were enough for McLaren to win its second consecutive title, and the third in its history.

With that, it looked like McLaren was beginning to establish its reign in Formula 1.

In 1986, Niki Lauda left Formula 1 for good, and his place at McLaren was taken by Keke Rosberg. The Finn had been champion in 1982 with TAG Williams Team. He remained with Williams for three more years, finishing fifth, eighth and third in the drivers' championship.

With his move to McLaren and the power of the MP4/2, he was confident he could become champion again. Alongside Prost, the McLaren team had two very talented drivers with the aim of continuing to maintain its dominance in Formula 1.

---

[38] 60years.autosport.com

The season did not start well for McLaren, with both drivers retiring in Brazil, but after a third place in Spain, Alain Prost managed to win the next two races: San Marino and Monaco. This allowed them to dream of a new year of dominance.

However, they were up against a tough opponent, Nigel Mansell's Williams FW11, which won four of the next five races, with Alain Prost taking four podiums to try to rival a surprisingly strong-performing Williams.

One of the main disadvantages of McLaren with respect to Williams was the high fuel consumption. Paradoxically, the power that had been gaining the TAG engine made it consume more than expected, which together with the limitation of 195 liters instead of 220 by the change of regulations suffered more than expected.

---

[39] F1-fansite.com

Mansell's winning streak slackened, achieving only one more victory in the second part of the season, mainly due to his teammate Nelson Piquet, who began to string together several wins.

This allowed Prost to compete against Mansell and Piquet for the drivers' championship until the final race in Australia. Although the French McLaren driver was at a disadvantage, a puncture by Mansell and a precautionary pit stop by Piquet allowed Alain Prost to win the Australian victory and become world champion again in a thrilling end to the season. He became only the second driver after Jack Brabham to win two consecutive world championships.

[40] Deviantart.com

McLaren thus won a new drivers' championship, but Keke Rosberg was unable to score enough points to beat the Williams of Mansell and Piquet.

Rosberg did not achieve any victory during the whole season, and only reached the podium in Monaco, finishing sixth in the final classification, so McLaren ceded the Formula 1 constructors' throne to Williams.

In 1987, McLaren lost Barnard for the MP4/3 design as the designer was leaving for Ferrari. Instead, they brought Steve Nichols, a development engineer from Hercules Aerospace, onto the development team.

The new car looked very different from the previous one, being lower and with a smaller nose to be less bulky in order to consume less fuel, and added side radiators.

[41] En.wheelsage.org

Leaving McLaren (and Formula 1) for this season was Keke Rosberg, who was replaced by Stefan Johansson to accompany Prost. The Swede was signed after being fifth in the standings in his second year with Ferrari. He had previously driven with incomplete programs at Toleman and Tyrrell in 1984, and at Spirit Racing in 1983.

Alain Prost won the first race in Brazil and the third in Belgium, with Johansson also taking podium finishes in both, which seemed to indicate that the MP4/3's settings were sufficient to beat the Williams.

However, as the season progressed, victory became increasingly distant, with wins being shared between the Williams of Mansell and Piquet and the Lotus of Ayrton Senna.

---

[42] Scuderiafans.com

In fact, Alain Prost only managed one more victory, in Portugal, seeing how the Williams was superior throughout the year, and was even behind Senna in the final standings.

For his part, Johansson was not able to win any race, although at least he managed to get on the podium five times. With this, McLaren managed to keep the runner-up position in the championship in the face of Lotus' push, but Williams once again snatched the constructors' championship, this time more comfortably.

The rivalry between Alain Prost and Ayrton Senna

In 1988, McLaren signed the talented Ayrton Senna to replace Johansson. The legendary Brazilian had made his Formula 1 debut in 1984, scoring three podiums with Toleman, one of the weakest teams on the grid.

After that he participated for three seasons with Lotus, finishing fourth in the final standings in the first two and third in the last one.

McLaren had two very talented drivers this season, who would end up becoming great rivals.

The main change in the new MP4/4 was the abandonment of Porsche engines, which had become obsolete, for Honda engines that had powered the invincible Williams of the previous season. McLaren adopted the 1.5L Honda V6 turbo engine, despite the fact that the rest of the teams were starting to install naturally aspirated engines, which would be mandatory by regulation from the following season, and that to encourage the transition the regulations penalized turbo engines.

The season was exceptional for McLaren, with an overwhelming dominance, winning 15 of the 16 races of the championship. In the only race they failed to win, Senna was leading when he crashed into a car he was lapping.

---

[43] Formulaf1.es

With this overwhelming dominance and no opponents for the all-powerful McLaren, the team's two drivers in turn became its only rivals. They were the only ones capable of beating each other, which generated a great rivalry between Prost and Senna. In Portugal, Senna pushed Prost into the pitlane wall, although the Frenchman was eventually able to win the race.

Prost won 7 races during the season and Senna won 8. Although the Frenchman accumulated more points than the Brazilian, the rule that only the 11 best performances scored points allowed Ayrton Senna to win his first drivers' championship.

McLaren, 134 points ahead of Ferrari, won its fourth constructors' championship comfortably.

44

In 1989, McLaren had to adapt to the turbo ban. To do so, Honda supplied a naturally aspirated 3.5L V10 engine.

---

[44] Laguiaformulera.com

The MP4/5 was very similar to its predecessor, and its main change besides the engine was the switch from longitudinal to transverse drive mid-season and for the following year.

Although the first race in Brazil was won by Nigel Mansell's Ferrari, the engine change did not seem to affect McLaren, which again dominated the season, taking 10 wins in the year's 16 races to add another constructors' title.

Once again, Senna and Prost were teammates and at the same time the only candidates for the title, which further intensified their rivalry. At San Marino, Senna breached the team agreement not to overtake at the first corner, which made Prost feel wronged and less valued, which is why he decided to join Ferrari for the following season.

In the final race in Japan, both drivers arrived with championship chances, which further escalated the hostilities. Both collided during the course of the race and although Senna was able to recover from the impact and win the race, he was eventually disqualified, giving the world championship to Alain Prost.

[45] Autobild.com

In 1990, Prost made good on his threat to join Ferrari, so it was Austrian Gerhard Berger who joined Senna at McLaren. Berger had driven for Ferrari for three years with a third place in the world championship as his best result, and before that he had participated one season with Benetton and another with Arrows.

[46]

Despite Prost's change of team, the season was once again a battle between the Frenchman and Ayrton Senna. The Brazilian won the first race in the United States, but Prost responded by winning the second race in Brazil.

The two went on to share the victories, with Senna accumulating six over the course of the year and Prost five.

---

[46] Sportphotogallery.com

This time the championship between the two was settled in the penultimate race in Japan. But it ended in the same way as the previous season: Senna crashed into Prost. However, this time the Brazilian was not penalized, and with both out of the race, Ayrton Senna was proclaimed world champion for the second time.

47

As for Gerhard Berger, he did not manage to win any race, but with 7 podiums and 43 points he allowed McLaren to beat Ferrari by 11 points, thus adding the sixth constructors' championship for the team, which was living its most glorious period.

1991 was presented without many changes beyond the new Honda V12 engine for the MP4/6, an engine that was not very powerful in its first tests, but that together with the talent of Ayrton Senna allowed the Brazilian to win the first four races of the season.

With this start, it looked like it was going to be a year of easy domination for McLaren and Senna, who reigned supreme in

---

[47] Diariovasco.com

Formula 1, especially with Prost struggling to win races (he didn't win all year).

However, as Williams' Renault RS3 engine became more reliable, the Canon Williams Team went on to dominate the championship, with Nigel Mansell taking three consecutive wins in France, Great Britain and Germany.

Senna reacted in time by winning the next two races in Hungary and Belgium, but Mansell came back in Italy and Spain.

Although the power of the Williams threatened McLaren's dominance, Senna finished the season with a second place in Japan and a victory in Australia to win his third championship with a comfortable final lead over Mansell of 24 points.

---

[48] Soymotor.com

Berger, who this time did manage to win a race in Japan, finished fourth in the final standings to help McLaren win its seventh constructors' title, extending its glory days.

In 1992, McLaren was confident of continuing to enjoy its dominance in Formula 1, however Mansell's Williams continued to progress and improved so much that it became the dominant car, with Mansell winning the first 5 races, and taking a total of eight wins in the first ten events of the year.

This made McLaren decide to bring forward the launch of the MP4/7 as soon as possible. It featured a semi-automatic gearbox, allowing you to keep your foot on the pedal without lifting it during gear changes.

This allowed Senna to win in Monaco, Hungary and Italy, but this was not enough to compete with the Williams of Mansell and Patrese, and the Brazilian even fell behind Michael Schumacher's Benetton in the final standings.

---

[49] Autolimite.com

Berger, paradoxically, improved on his previous results, with two wins and three podium finishes that saw him finish fourth in the world championship, just one point behind Senna.

As a team, they managed to keep the runner-up position 8 points ahead of Benetton, but they were far behind Williams, who snatched the first place they had become accustomed to in Woking.

The era of McLaren's dominance in Formula 1 was thus broken.

In 1993, Honda withdrew from Formula 1 to participate in IndyCar, so McLaren went back to Ford engines, using the Ford HBE7 3.5 V8, although it had tried unsuccessfully to negotiate for the Renault engine that was giving Williams so much power.

Berger was signed by Ferrari, so McLaren signed Michael Andretti as Senna's teammate. Michael had won the IndyCar in 1991, but had no Formula 1 experience.

[50]

In 1993, Nigel Mansell participated in the IndyCar (becoming champion), and his seat in Williams was occupied by Alain Prost. This

---

[50] Thebestf1.es

meant that Senna was once again facing his former teammate, now with favorable conditions for the Frenchman due to the potential of the Williams.

In fact, it was Prost who won the first race in South Africa, but Senna won the next two. The Frenchman won the fourth and fifth races, and Senna won the sixth in an exchange of victories that rekindled the rivalry between the two.

Then it was Alain Prost who won four consecutive races in Canada, France, Great Britain and Germany, tipping the balance in his favor. After this series of triumphs, it was his teammate Damon Hill who achieved three consecutive victories in what established Williams' dominance.

Senna reacted at the end of the season with the two final victories in Japan and Australia, but they came too late to overtake Prost and the Brazilian had to settle for the runner-up position.

Michael Andretti did not have a good campaign, retiring in the first four races, and obtaining a single podium in Italy. This led to Finnish Mika Häkkinen replacing him in the last three events. Häkkinen came

---

[51] Diariomotor.com

to McLaren after two years at Lotus as Formula 1 experience where he had scored 2 points in the first season and 11 in the second.

Häkkinen retired in two of the three races in which he participated, but in Japan he managed to get on the podium.

With this, McLaren was once again runner-up in the constructors' championship, but was still far behind Williams, which doubled its points tally.

---

[52] F1-fansite.com

Senna's farewell and the beginning of McLaren-Mercedes era

In 1994, Ayrton Senna signed for Williams, which had become the car every driver wanted to drive. This was the season of his fateful accident in San Marino that caused Formula 1 to lose one of its most talented drivers in history.

Senna's departure to a rival team meant that McLaren lost its best driver, making it more difficult for the team to fight for another world championship.

Trying to find additional power to match Williams, the team negotiated with Lamborghini as an engine supplier, but after unsuccessful negotiations, the 760 horsepower Peugeot A6 3.5 V10 engine was finally used for the 1994 MP4/9.

The new single-seater was designed by Neil Oatley with the aim of reducing the differences with Williams. This year, assisted braking, active suspension, traction control and ABS were eliminated, with the aim of returning the protagonism to the drivers over the mechanical aids.

Häkkinen continued with the team after his three races in 1993, this time with a full program. His teammate was British driver Martin Brundle, who made his Formula 1 debut in 1984, driving for Tyrrell for three years before a season with West Zakspeed Racing. After that he participated for two years with Motor Racing Developments where he continued to score points frequently. In 1992 he was part of the Camel Benetton Ford structure, scoring his first podiums, a total of six, and in 1993 he added one more podium in the Ligier Gitanes Blondes.

McLaren therefore incorporated an experienced driver looking to regain the Formula 1 throne.

[53] Es.vmax.si

The season started with complications, with both cars retiring in the first two races, but Häkkinen gave the team hope with a podium finish in San Marino, the day the world lost Ayrton Senna.

The good result in San Marino was a mirage, as three more retirements followed for the Finn, although at least Brundle kept hope alive with a second place in Monaco.

The second half was more prosperous for McLaren, with Häkkinen scoring five more podiums despite an accident in Germany that also caused him to miss the Hungarian race where he was replaced by Frenchman Phillippe Alliot, who also eventually retired. Martin Brundle also scored one more podium in the last race in Australia.

This meant that Häkkinen could finish fourth in the drivers' championship and the Briton seventh, but a harsh reality was reached: it was the first time since 1980 that the McLaren had failed to win at least one race in a season.

In this way, not only was it impossible to catch up with Williams (who won the championship once again), but it remained behind Benetton and Ferrari in a clear and hard setback.

[54] Statsf1.com

In 1995, Peugeot left due to the poor reliability of its engine, and McLaren began to be powered by Mercedes-Benz engines, designed by Ilmor.

The MP4/10 was powered by the Mercedes FO 110 3.0 V10. The main feature of the single-seater was the needle-nosed nose, which radically changed the look of Formula 1.

The car's test performance was promising, which rekindled the team's hopes. This optimism was compounded by the signing of former champion Nigel Mansell. However, the Briton could not fit in the cockpit, which caused him pain in his hips and elbows, so he could not participate in the first two races while the car was being adapted.

---

[55] Carpixel.net

Häkkinen started the season alongside Briton Mark Blundell, who had finished 13th with Tyrrell the previous season, scoring a single podium in Spain. Prior to that, he had driven for Ligier for one season, scoring two podiums, and had made his Formula 1 debut with Motor Racing Developments in 1991.

[56]

Häkkinen started the season fourth in Brazil and retired in Argentina, while Blundell was sixth in the first race and also retired in the second.

For San Marino and Spain the desired arrival of Mansell was confirmed, but after finishing tenth in the first and retiring in the second, and not feeling comfortable with the car, he left the program, with Blundell returning as second driver.

The rest of the season was quite inconsistent, although Häkkinen achieved two podiums and Blundell one, and both were able to score points repeatedly, the retirements were still many and McLaren failed to be a consistent team. Häkkinen finished seventh in the world championship and the Briton in 13th position.

---

[56] Aminoapps.com

Overall, McLaren finished fourth and was overtaken by the champion Benetton, by Williams and by Ferrari, moving away from the high positions it had occupied in previous years.

In 1996, the MP4/11 was developed with the help of Alain Prost as a consultant, due to the absence of Häkkinen who had suffered a serious accident in qualifying in Australia in the previous campaign. In the second year of partnership with Mercedes, the aim was to improve on the previous disappointing season.

Häkkinen's teammate on this occasion was the British David Coulthard. The Briton had debuted in 1994 with Williams in Formula 1, finishing eighth, and had been third in 1995 with the Rothmans Williams Renault. While waiting to see if the new McLaren could compete with Williams, at least they got one of their drivers.

[57]

---

[57] Racinghalloffamecollection.com

The season was similar to the previous one, with Häkkinen scoring points in almost every race and taking four podiums, and Coulthard adding two more podiums and also scoring points in another four races. The Finn finished fifth and the Briton seventh and between them they scored 49 points, putting McLaren in the same position as the previous year, fourth behind the main protagonists of the scene: the all-powerful Williams, Ferrari and Benetton-Renault.

McLaren remained winless for another year.

[58]

In 1997 Marlboro was abandoned after 23 years of association and the team was renamed to West McLaren Mercedes, acquiring a black and silver coloration according to the new sponsor.

Although the MP4/12 was very similar to its predecessor, it incorporated an innovative second brake pedal that allowed it to act on only one of the rear wheels, eliminating part of the understeer.

---

[58] Oneimagef1.wordpress.com

Mercedes' FO110E 3.0 V10 engines showed great promise, with Coulthard winning the inaugural race in Australia, with Häkkinen also taking a podium finish, and bringing McLaren back to the top in a Grand Prix.

The Finn scored points in the next three races, but Coulthard began to suffer from what would be the main problem of the season and which slowed down the team's evolution: engine reliability. The FO110E was replaced during the year by an improved version, the F0110F, but the reliability problems were not solved.

Even so, both Coulthard and Häkkinen managed to win one more race each, and the Briton finished second in two more races, enabling him to finish third in the world championship, three places ahead of his Finnish teammate.

Despite these new successes, McLaren was again in fourth place in the constructors' standings, mainly due to numerous retirements.

---

[59] Aminoapps.com

But at least, it was only 4 points behind Benetton, and with a new power that, if it could be controlled, could be the beginning of a new resurgence.

In 1998, McLaren counted on Adrian Newey to design the MP4/13. The engineer had helped Bobby Rahal succeed in IndyCar in 1986 and 1987. In Europe, he had worked with the March team, where he rose to the position of technical director because of his commitment to aerodynamics at a time when it was not a priority. Despite the team's progress, Newey was fired in 1990, but he had no trouble finding a position with a new team, joining Williams.

With more resources and equipment, Newey was able to deploy his talents at Williams to help the team become the dominant team in Formula 1. In 1998, McLaren hoped he could achieve the same with the Woking-based team.

[60]

Newey had already participated during the end of the previous season in the development of the single-seater, so this time his

---

[60] Safety-car.es

impact on the car by directing the design was greater and it was expected to make a leap in quality.

The MP4/13 was an almost entirely new car, adapting to the new regulations that generated thinner vehicles and used grooved wheels.

Newey's influence was quickly shown and McLaren achieved a one-two finish in the first race in Australia, with Häkkinen winning the race, a result that was repeated in Brazil.

Schumacher tried to stop McLaren's advance and the season became an even fight between Ferrari's German and Häkkinen.

The Finnish driver achieved 8 victories during the year, while Schumacher won 6 races. Both reached the end of the season evenly matched, but Häkkinen's two victories in the final races in Luxembourg and Japan allowed the Finn to become world champion.

---

[61] Carpixel.net

Coulthard, although he only achieved one victory and was third behind Schumacher, scored 8 podiums that helped McLaren to win the constructors' world championship, achieving the eighth world title in its history.

For 1999, Newey continued to enhance the aerodynamics of the MP4/14, and the Mercedes engine was confirmed as the most powerful on the grid, which made McLaren dream of a new era of dominance in the competition, despite the fact that it had been banned from using the independent braking system.

The season was similar to the previous one. Häkkinen continued to achieve frequent victories with the best car on the grid, but he had to fight very intensely with a Ferrari, which this year would not be that of Michael Schumacher who suffered a severe accident in Great Britain that left him out of six races.

His main rival was Eddie Irvine. Both shared the victories throughout the year, and in fact the British driver had the advantage at the last

---

[62] Thelastcorner.it

race in Japan. However, Häkkinen achieved a decisive victory in the last race which, together with Irvine's third place, was enough to win his second consecutive title, only 2 points ahead of Eddie.

However, this time Coulthard's fourth place and 48 points were not enough to keep the constructors' title. Although the Briton did achieve two victories during the year, it was not enough to prevent Ferrari from snatching the constructors' title.

In 2000, the battle between McLaren and Ferrari was once again revived, personified mainly in the duel between Häkkinen and Schumacher.

The German, recovered from his injuries, came back stronger than ever and in a brilliant season, he hardly left any options, winning 9 races throughout the year. Häkkinen, on the other hand, could only obtain 4 victories, which made him settle for the runner-up position.

---

[63] Automundo.com.ar

Although Coulthard was third in the world championship, Schumacher's superiority was such that together with Barrichello's fourth place, Ferrari managed to keep the constructors' championship. In addition, McLaren was deducted 10 points for not presenting one of the stamps required by the FIA in Austria.

In 2001, the Mercedes engines began to be less powerful than the BMW engines used by Williams, aerodynamic resources were less effective on the MP4/16 and driver assistance systems were not successfully implemented.

This made it difficult for Häkkinen to maintain his performance, taking his first win after 11 races and only managing two victories all year.

On the other hand, Coulthard progressed and replaced the Finn. Although he also won two victories, he was on the podium many more times with a regularity that allowed him to be runner-up in the

---

[64] F1-fansite.com

drivers' standings, although he obtained little more than half the points of Schumacher, who was still reigning in Formula 1.

Häkkinen finished fifth in a remarkable drop in performance that caused him to leave Formula 1, ending his long partnership with Coulthard in the McLaren team.

As for the constructors' world championship, McLaren once again achieved a new runner-up position, although instead of closing the gap with the dominant Ferrari, it looked back to a dangerous BMW-Williams, which improved significantly.

---

[65] Maxf1.net

In 2002, Häkkinen was replaced by another Finn, Kimi Räikkönen, who had debuted the previous season with the Sauber team, scoring 9 points and demonstrating great talent despite his youth.

[66]

The MP4/17 did not perform as expected, but both Coulthard and Räikkönen performed to score podium finishes 5 and 4 times respectively, to finish fifth and sixth in the drivers' championship.

---

[66] Wykop.pl

However, no victory was achieved throughout the season and while Ferrari continued to dominate at Schumacher's pace, Williams also overtook McLaren in the constructors' standings, relegating the team to third place.

In 2003, an evolution of the MP4/17 showed great promise, with Coulthard winning the first race and Räikkönen the second.

However, Schumacher continued to impose his infinite talent and achieved three consecutive victories in San Marino, Spain and Austria, to further establish Ferrari's dominance.

Although Kimi did not win again, he did climb the podium repeatedly, putting Schumacher under pressure until the end and finishing second in the championship, just two points behind the German, who won his sixth world championship.

---

[67] Scuderiafans.com

Despite Räikkönen's resistance, Coulthard did not have a great season, after his season-opening victory in Australia, he only managed one more podium finish in the last race in Japan.

This allowed Williams to move ahead by only two points, and despite initial optimism, McLaren was back in third place in the constructors' championship.

In 2004, the MP4/19 was used directly, following a disappointing MP4/18 that had failed the crash tests. This new single-seater was a corrected version of the MP4/18 that conformed to the new regulations prohibiting launch control and fully automatic gears.

From Spain onwards, it was replaced by an MP4/19B showing a completely different aerodynamic package.

[68] Scuderiafans.com

The car proved very uncompetitive, with Räikkönen retiring in the first three races and Coulthard struggling to score points.

This dynamic was repeated throughout the first half of the championship. With the arrival of the MP4/19B, results improved slightly, and Kimi was even able to achieve the team's only victory of the season, in Belgium.

However, this drop in performance made it impossible to try to fight with Ferrari and Williams, and also fell behind BAR-Honda and Renault. McLaren was fifth in the constructors' championship, its worst result since 1983.

---

[69] Neumaticointermedio.com

Following recent failures, the MP4/20 chassis was completely redesigned. The diffuser was smaller, the front wing was higher and the rear wing had a more forward position, as well as characteristic small wings on the bodywork.

Coulthard left the team after 9 years with the team, and was replaced by Colombian Juan Pablo Montoya. Montoya had been IndyCar champion in 1999, and had driven for Williams between 2001 and 2004, finishing third in the championship twice. Injured, he had to be replaced in the third race by the Spaniard Pedro de la Rosa and in the fourth by the Austrian Alexander Wurz, but was able to complete the rest of the season.

---

[70] Snaplap.net

[71]

Although the season started mediocrely, with McLaren struggling for points, from Spain onwards the tide turned radically, with Räikkönen starting to win races frequently.

Meanwhile, Fernando Alonso, who had started the season in an unexpected and impressive way with 6 victories in 11 races, began to have difficulties to get back to winning ways.

Kimi's upward dynamic and Fernando's stagnation meant that both were fighting for the drivers' championship. McLaren was once again in contention for a world title. However, the McLaren proved to be less reliable, which cost the Finnish driver having to retire in races he was leading and finally, together with the tire heating problem that hurt qualifying, he was finally unable to overtake the Spaniard.

Montoya, despite missing two races, finished fourth in the competition with three victories, but only scored two points more

[71] F1-fansite.com

than Fisichella, Alonso's teammate at Renault, so the constructors' title went to the French team.

At least McLaren once again felt capable of fighting for a championship.

With that goal in mind, the Emirates-sponsored MP4-21 was developed in 2006 for the team, which was renamed simply Team McLaren Mercedes. The aim was to achieve greater reliability, which would have helped Kimi to become champion in the previous season... but in return, power suffered.

This prevented the team from achieving victories in a championship monopolized by the fight between Fernando Alonso and Michael Schumacher, but at least the McLarens were able to score points easily and achieve some podiums.

Meanwhile, the relationship between their two drivers became more strained and in the United States the two McLarens collided with

---

[72] Thebestf1.es

each other, causing Montoya to finally decide to leave the team to participate in NASCAR.

For the last 8 races, Montoya was replaced by Spaniard Pedro de la Rosa, who had already driven for McLaren in one race in 2005, and had previously participated two seasons at Jaguar after two years at Arrows. In eight appearances this year with McLaren, he scored one podium and four points.

73

Räikkönen finished fifth in a season in which not a single race was won, something that had not happened in ten years. With no chance of victory, the Finn signed for Ferrari for the following season.

---

[73] Thebestf1.es

McLaren finished third, far behind Renault and Ferrari, which meant a step backwards whose cause seemed to be internal instability, with Adrian Newey frequently considering leaving the structure.

McLaren needed to find a new balance if it wanted to remain at the top of Formula 1.

Hamilton's arrival and Spygate

In 2007, McLaren renewed its driver line-up and signed Fernando Alonso, thus securing the services of the recent two-time champion and the best driver of the moment.

The Spaniard had made his debut at Minardi in 2001 before spending six years at Renault (the first as a test driver), winning the world title in the last two, and leading the French team to its first-ever constructors' championship.

The team's second driver was rookie Lewis Hamilton, who had just won the GP2 Series. Ron Dennis had met him at a karting event when Lewis was just 10 years old, and even as a young boy, Hamilton approached him and asked if he could give him his phone number.

Since then, Ron Dennis had been attentive and had taken care of his progress until his arrival in Formula 1, where in his first year in the competition he gave him a seat in the team.

McLaren therefore had a team made up of an experienced two-time champion and an up-and-coming talent, who soon proved to be more of a present talent.

The MP4-22 was designed without Adrian Newey, by the team formed by Neil Oatley, Paddy Lowe, Mike Coughlan, Pat Fry and Simon Lacey. It incorporated novel aerodynamic elements such as a carbon fiber top arching over the nose.

[74]

The new Mclaren was very competitive, resuming its old rivalry with Ferrari. Ferrari drivers Räikkönen and Felipe Massa won three of the first five races, with Alonso triumphing in the remaining two.

Meanwhile, Hamilton was on the podium in all those races, showing his potential and shed his rookie tag by winning the races in Canada and the United States and joining the fight for the championship.

---

[74] Thebestf1.es

Victories continued to be shared among the four protagonists (no other driver won any race that season), but in addition to Ferrari, McLaren found a new enemy within its own structure. Their two drivers were showing an increasingly strained relationship with each other.

In Hungary, the FIA accused Alonso of deliberately disadvantaging his teammate in qualifying, for which the team was penalized with no points in that race. Both drivers also failed to reach an agreement to have an extra lap in qualifying alternately throughout the season and to have equal opportunities in the Saturday session throughout the season.

The equality in the championship until the last race in Brazil (Kimi had won five races, Lewis four and Fernando another four), meant that up to three drivers had options to become champions in the last Grand Prix.

Hamilton started with a 4-point lead over Alonso and a 7-point lead over Räikkönen, but gearbox problems caused him to finish seventh.

The battle was then between Kimi and Alonso, but the Finn was the fastest, winning the race and with his teammate Massa in second place, Alonso finished third and the drivers' world championship slipped away from McLaren.

---

[75] Faz.net

However, overall, Hamilton and Alonso scored more points than Kimi and Massa, so there was still the consolation of the constructors' world championship... except that *Spygate* broke out: the McLaren team was accused of spying and deliberately copying the Ferrari team.

The FIA ruled that McLaren had technical documents patented by Ferrari and had taken advantage of them, so it was disqualified as a team and relegated to the last position, being also sanctioned with a fine of 100 million euros.

For the 2008 season, Alonso's dissatisfaction materialized with his departure to Renault, after considering that McLaren gave favored treatment to Hamilton. He was replaced by the Finnish Heikki Kovalainen, who in 2007 had made his Formula 1 debut with the Renault team, achieving a podium and finishing in seventh position.

The MP4-23 was developed under strict FIA surveillance so that no information from Ferrari's stolen documentation was used. This year's regulations prohibited traction control. The wheelbase was

---

[76] F1history.fandom.com

increased. The "shark fin" was incorporated as an aerodynamic element, although as it did not prove to be effective, it was eventually withdrawn. From the Hungarian Grand Prix onwards, the "Dumbo wings" were incorporated in the nose.

Despite the strict need to forcibly redesign the McLaren due to *Spygate*, the new car proved just as competitive with Hamilton winning the first race in Australia. The next four went to the Ferraris, with Massa taking two wins and Kimi two, but Lewis returned to victory in Monaco.

The fight between McLaren and Ferrari was reproduced throughout the season, although reduced to Hamilton and Massa, who disputed the drivers' championship.

By the final race in Brazil, Hamilton had a seven-point lead over Massa. The Brazilian did his job and led the race, forcing Hamilton to finish fifth if he was to win his first world championship.

---

[77] Deporteyocio.es

Before the final lap, Lewis was sixth, but an overtake on the final corner and in the midst of the confusion, he got the fifth place he needed to become world champion in dramatic fashion.

78

Heikki Kovalainen, although he got the victory in Hungary and two more podiums, was seventh in the final classification, far behind Räikkönen who was third, so the constructors' world championship went to Ferrari.

In 2009, Ron Dennis left the position of general manager, and this position was filled by Martin Whitmarsh. Hamilton and Kovalainen were retained for an MP4-24 that proved to be the worst car in pre-season testing, occupying the last positions in the timesheets.

79

---

[78] Maxf1.net
[79] Autoviva.es

The poor forecasts for the MP4-24 were confirmed, with McLaren unable to score any podium finishes in the first half of the season.

From Malaysia onwards, the team incorporated the controversial double diffuser that had made the new Brawn GP team's car unbeatable.

The teams had complained that it was in breach of the regulations, but the FIA finally considered it legal and all the teams gradually incorporated it, although it was too late to compete against a Brawn that had already scored a lot of points in the first races.

Along with the double diffuser and other aerodynamic tweaks, McLaren improved in the second half of the championship, with Hamilton taking two wins and three podiums to climb to fifth in the final driver standings.

Kovalainen, thanks to the improvements, managed to score more often, but he did not even achieve any podium during the whole year, finishing in 12th position.

Despite the poor performance of the car, McLaren managed to move one point ahead of Ferrari to take third place in the constructors' championship, albeit with half the points of Red Bull and well behind the controversial Brawn.

The split of McLaren - Mercedes

In 2010, McLaren ceased to be the official Mercedes team. The German brand, after buying the Brawn GP team, created its own team, so McLaren, which had already seen how Mercedes motorized the champion team in the previous season, became just another customer and the strong and successful partnership between the two was limited and the relationship began to break up, with Mercedes selling part of its shares in McLaren.

To replace Heikki Kovalainen, who went on to drive for Lotus, McLaren signed British driver Jenson Button. Button had made his debut in 2000 with BMW Williams, from where he went on to drive for Renault for two seasons. After that he had a long relationship with Honda where he achieved his first victory in 2006 and his best final position in a Formula 1 World Championship: third in 2004.

His signing with Brawn in 2009 allowed him to win a world championship tainted by the controversy of regulatory permissiveness, and in McLaren he had a chance to continue to show his great quality.

The design of the MP4-25 was not without controversy, with an air intake in front of the driver that channeled the wind towards the rear wing, causing it to move by the thrust of the air giving it an aerodynamic improvement, which was denounced by Red Bull as the regulations did not allow moving aerodynamic elements.

This movable rear wing system was inspected by the FIA and found to be fully legal.

Hamilton scored a podium finish in the first race of the season in Bahrain and Button won the second race in Australia, which made it possible to be optimistic about the car's performance.

The wins kept coming, with Hamilton taking three victories and Button adding one more win, and getting on the podium more often than not. However, one rival was standing out above the rest in the championship, Red Bull, which seemed impossible to catch with Webber and Vettel winning 9 races in the season.

Alonso, who scored five wins with Ferrari, also finished ahead of the McLaren drivers.

The McLaren team's 454 points, although 44 fewer than Red Bull's, were enough to clinch the constructors' runner-up spot, end the uncertainty of the previous year and return McLaren to the top of the table.

In 2011, Hamilton and Button were still the team's starting drivers, hoping to get that little bit of extra performance that would allow them to overtake Red Bull. To this end, the MP4-26 incorporated novel high L-shaped pontoons to draw more air into a rear wing that was also narrower in order to carry the flow to the single rear diffuser, following the ban on the use of the twin diffuser.

Although the goal was to catch Red Bull, the energy drinks team proved even more challenging than the previous season, and in the hands of a talented Vettel, who scored a total of 11 victories, it was impossible to compete for the drivers' title.

Button, at least, managed to win the personal battle against Mark Webber's Red Bull. With three victories and 9 podiums, the Briton managed to finish runner-up in the drivers' championship.

Hamilton, although he also achieved three victories, finished fifth in the drivers' standings, mainly due to points lost due to on-track incidents with other drivers, mainly Felipe Massa.

Red Bull's superiority meant that McLaren was 153 points behind the champion team and had to settle for being once again the best of the rest.

---

[80] Motor.es

In 2012, the single-seater designs were characterized by the "duck nose", but McLaren was one of three teams that did not incorporate this characteristic shape, opting for a gradual slope in the nose.

It thus differentiated itself from Red Bull, in the hope of finally being able to be superior to its main rival.

[81]

Button won the first race of the season, with Hamilton third, allowing the team to be optimistic about overtaking Red Bull.

The second victory came in the seventh race, in Canada, this time through Hamilton. The distribution of victories was also extended to Ferrari through Alonso, and Räikkönen, although he did not achieve any victory, also remained at the top thanks to his regularity with a surprising Lotus.

This put the championship back on a level playing field... until Red Bull showed great development of its car throughout the year to

---

[81] Pinterest.com

once again dominate as it had done before, with Vettel winning four consecutive races in Singapore, Japan, Korea and India.

Despite this, Vettel still had to fight very evenly with Alonso to add a new title while McLaren, although they continued to get victories as Hamilton in the penultimate race in the United States and Button in the last race in Brazil (equaling Red Bull with 7 victories), were out of the fight.

In this way, not only was it unable to compete against Red Bull, but it also fell behind Ferrari, dropping to third place in the constructors' world championship.

In 2013, Lewis Hamilton left McLaren to join the Mercedes team in a very wise personal decision that would lead him to win six world championships.

The British driver was replaced by Mexican Sergio Pérez. Checo" had two seasons in Formula 1 with the Sauber team, achieving 3 podiums in his second year, finishing in tenth position in the final drivers' standings.

The MP4-28, in its sixth year of partnership with Vodafone, was a significant departure from the previous car, which had been terminated from development. The suspensions were completely

---

[82] Carburando.com

different, with a fork-shaped rear suspension capable of varying the tire arrangement according to speed to reduce wear. The pontoons were changed to improve air flow, and the front end was noticeably raised compared to the previous year's design. Although externally the single-seater was very similar to the 2012 car, internally it was a car with many changes.

With this, McLaren hoped to end its downward trend and be able to fight for championships again. But the reality was quite different.

The season started with both McLarens fighting for points, but always far from the podium.

In fact, no podium finishes were achieved, something that had not happened since 1980, in what was considered a dramatic season of

---

[83] Carpixel.net

complete failure. The best McLaren finish was Jenson Button's fourth place in Brazil.

The Briton scored a total of 73 points, finishing ninth in the final standings, and Perez finished 11th with 49 points. McLaren dropped to a dismal fifth position in the constructors' world championship.

After the disaster of 2013, Ron Dennis returned to team management. Checo Pérez was replaced by Kevin Magnussen to accompany Button. The Dane was making his Formula 1 debut after winning the Formula Renault 3.5 Series.

The MP4-29 reinstated the turbo engine that had not been used since 1988 and with which Prost and Senna had triumphed in the glorious McLaren years that now seemed very distant.

Magnussen debuted with a second position in Australia, accompanied on the podium by Button who was third. Both McLarens were on the podium (thanks to Ricciardo's disqualification) and this allowed to be optimistic about the future.

However, this turned out to be a false hope as the team failed to score another podium finish all season, although they managed to at

---

[84] Autobild.com

least score points in almost every race, with Button finishing a few places ahead of Magnussen on a regular basis.

Jenson Button finished eighth with 126 points and Magnussen 11th with 55 points, giving the McLaren team fifth place again in a year that did not substantially improve on the previous season's poor performance, but at least served as a parachute to avoid continuing the downward trend.

---

[85] Revistadelmotor.es

The McLaren-Honda era

For the 2015 season, the partnership between McLaren and Mercedes came to an end, with the British team acquiring 40% of the shares still held by the German brand.

Honda became the engine supplier of a McLaren that abandoned the silver color to paint the car black, hoping that the future of this new partnership would not be so dark.

Kevin Magnussen was relegated to test driver after the return of Fernando Alonso, who after two years at Renault and five at Ferrari, where he won three runner-up positions, was returning to the Woking team.

Autobild.com

However, a concussion meant that Alonso was unable to take part in the first race of the season, being replaced by Magnussen.

The Honda RA615H engine powered the MP4-30 after twenty years of using Mercedes engines. The single-seater was characterized by its tapered rear end designed to allow the Honda engine to operate at higher temperatures than in the other cars.

However, this new partnership with Honda did not start as expected. It took six races to score points, with Button's eighth place in Monaco. The Briton only managed to score points in three more races, scoring 16 points at the end of the year, and Alonso only scored 11 points between Great Britain and Hungary, in the latter race finishing fifth and achieving McLaren's best result of the season.

McLaren finished second to last in the constructors' standings, just ahead of the Marussia team, in a terrible year that marked a major decline of a historic team.

In 2016, the MP4-31 improved its test results, mainly due to the development of the Honda engine that had been blamed for poor performance in the previous campaign.

Button and Alonso continued as the first drivers, although the Spaniard suffered a severe accident in the first race in Australia that caused him to fracture several ribs and lung damage.

---

[87] Autosport.com

This led to him being replaced by reserve driver Stoffel Vandoorne in Bahrain, who made a successful debut, finishing tenth and scoring the first points for the team.

The rest of the year, it was a conformist season where they managed to score points again frequently, in a slight improvement over the previous campaign. Alonso managed to score 54 points to finish tenth, and Button scored 21 points, finishing 15th. McLaren's best position this season was Alonso's fifth place in Monaco and the United States, in another year far from the podium but at least an evolution from the terrible previous season, moving up to sixth position in the constructors' championship.

In 2017, McLaren continued to rely on Honda, hoping that its engine would continue to evolve as much as it had done the previous season, to be able to at least compete for podiums in this season. For the development of the RA617H engine, the token-based development system was eliminated and Honda therefore had greater freedom to evolve its engine.

---

[88] Soymotor.com

Button left the team after 8 seasons at McLaren, although he would return to replace Fernando Alonso in Monaco, as the Spaniard was competing in the Indianapolis 500.

McLaren's second driver this season was Belgian Stoffel Vandoorne, who had convinced the team after replacing Fernando the previous season, scoring points on his debut.

The start of the season highlighted the reliability of the Honda engine, with Alonso retiring in the first two races, and the withdrawals being replicated throughout the year, such as the double retirement in China, Monaco and Italy.

In the races he did manage to finish, he was not very competitive either, placing between eighth and tenth to score a few consolation points.

---

[89] Fast-mag.com

Alonso finished 15th with 17 points and Vandoorne 16th with 13 points, putting McLaren back in second-to-last place in the constructors' standings, only ahead of Sauber.

This new failure led to a loss of confidence in the Honda engine and ended the partnership with the Japanese engine manufacturer.

The McLaren-Renault era

For 2018 and after assuming the Honda partnership era as a disastrous stage in its history, McLaren signed a contract with Renault as engine supplier for three years. For this new stage, it was returning to the old papaya color as the main coloring of the single-seater.

Vandoorne and Alonso repeated in the driver lineup for an MCL33 that had development problems from the start. Tim Goss, as technical director, had the objective of creating a chassis adapted to the new engine. The position of the turbo conflicted with the gearbox, so its layout had to be changed, as well as the engine bay itself and the rear suspension.

The introduction of the halo also meant that the chassis had to be substantially modified, so the MCL33 was an almost completely rebuilt car.

Alonso achieved an encouraging fifth place in the first race in Australia, which showed a clear improvement in this new stage with Renault. However, this was the best result of a season that was disappointing in each race.

Throughout the year, the McLaren managed to score on several occasions with difficulties, with Alonso occupying seventh and eighth place as the most repeated result, and Vandoorne with many difficulties to overcome the tenth place, scoring in only four of the 21 races.

These poor results were mainly due to poor qualifying sessions on Saturdays, where they only managed to stay ahead of Williams. The one-lap performance of the MCL33 was very poor and conditioned the Sunday results, with McLaren reaching sixth position in the constructors' championship (after Force India's disqualification due to licensing problems).

---

[90] Beinsports.com

The previous disastrous seasons were improved upon, but there was little room for optimism in the new partnership with Renault.

Alonso, after this season in which he finished 11th with 50 points, decided to retire from Formula 1 to pursue other disciplines, before returning in 2021 with Alpine.

Vandoorne, 16th with 12 points, also left the team to continue his Formula E career.

For 2019, McLaren completely renewed its driver line-up. One of those joining the team was Carlos Sainz Jr. The Spaniard had debuted at Toro Rosso in 2015 after winning the Formula Renault 3.5 Series, where he drove for two and a half years, with a 12th place as the best final position in the drivers' standings.

The last part of 2017 he finished at Renault, a team with which in 2018 he enjoyed a full program while being a test driver for McLaren. In 2019, he would become a regular driver for the Woking-based team.

---

[91] Lawebdelmotor.es

His teammate was Briton Lando Norris, also a test driver in 2018, a year in which he finished second in the Formula 2 championship. McLaren thus had a squad of young drivers in the second year of its partnership with Renault.

For this season Renault supplied the new Renault E-Tech 19, after coming to terms with the failure of its transition to the hybrid era, in an engine model that was intended to better adapt to the use of extra electric power.

With the departure of Tim Goss, Peter Prodromou was put in charge of the MCL34 design. Pat Fry also returned to the British team after his time at Ferrari and also joined James Key from Toro Rosso.

---

[92] Autobild.com

The new car was a positive surprise. It could not compete with Ferrari, Red Bull, and much less with the almighty Mercedes of the hybrid era, but it did consolidate itself as the best of the rest, an honor that was supposed to go to the team that supplied the engines: Renault.

Both drivers managed to score points frequently, and even Carlos Sainz managed a third place in Brazil that returned a McLaren that had not achieved it since 2014 to the podium (although it had officially finished fourth, a post-race penalty on Hamilton allowed the final third place that could not be properly celebrated).

Sainz finished the season sixth with 96 points and Lando Norris made his Formula 1 debut in 11th place with 49 points. Overall, McLaren moved up to fourth place and was encouraged by a progressive evolution in the partnership with Renault engines.

---

[93] Actualidadmotor.com

For the 2020 season, McLaren retained Sainz and Norris, and significantly evolved the MCL35 in the hope of continuing the positive trend that would return McLaren to the fight for victories.

The main changes were aimed at further optimizing the chassis to the Renault engine and improving cornering ability, with aerodynamic innovations that sought to get the airflow around the tire rather than over it. The side pontoons were made thinner to improve cooling and the nose was made thinner.

The goal of the development team was to emphasize the function of each part in the whole assembly, rather than looking for the best possible independent parts and then assembling them.

At the beginning of the season, the coronavirus pandemic burst in, affecting the organization of Formula 1 and the sport in general,

---

[94] F1enestadopuro.com

forcing a restructuring of the calendar with double races at the same circuits, adapting to the health situation of each nationality and implementing new protocols in each Grand Prix.

Economically, it meant a great loss for the teams, mainly due to the fact that most of the races had to be held without spectators.

But despite the health circumstances, McLaren was able to continue the positive trend of the previous year. This time there were two podiums achieved by the team during the year. Lando Norris achieved the first of them in the opening race in Austria, and Carlos the second in Monza, where he finished second and could even have taken the victory if the race had lasted a few laps longer, catching up lap after lap with Pierre Gasly, who surprisingly took the win.

Sainz finished sixth again and Norris improved his position from the previous year by finishing ninth. In the constructors' world championship, McLaren made the most of its 202 points to move up to third position, only surpassed by Red Bull and Mercedes, which dominated Formula 1.

---

[95] Elprogreso.es

The return to Mercedes engines and the future

The new season was agreed to be a repeat of 2020. A revolutionary change in the regulations was planned for 2021, but after the economic disaster caused by the pandemic and in order to reduce costs, it was decided to use the same single-seaters for another year.

Although the chassis was the same, McLaren took advantage of the end of its contract with Renault to opt for a new engine supplier: Mercedes. It thus obtained the Mercedes-AMG engine that had led the German team to win the last seven constructors' championships.

Carlos Sainz, meanwhile, signed for Ferrari, so McLaren opted for Daniel Ricciardo to accompany Lando Norris. The Australian already had a long and experienced career in Formula 1 since he debuted at HRT in 2011 to go on to drive for Toro Rosso for two seasons before moving up to Red Bull, a team with which he participated for five years, twice finishing third in the final position in the constructors' championship.

In 2019 and 2020 he was a Renault driver, helping the French team to return to the podium again, a complicated bet that the Australian finally came to fruition (with tattoo in between).

[96]

McLaren's upward trajectory of recent years continued on this occasion, mainly due to the evolution of Lando Norris as a driver, who achieved three podiums in the first nine races.

The euphoria subsided as the Briton never again stood on the podium, although through great qualifying sessions (achieving McLaren's first pole position in the hybrid era), he managed to score points in 20 of the year's 22 races, albeit in lower and lower positions as the season progressed.

---

[96] F1-fansite.com

In the end, Norris scored 160 points to move up to fifth in the constructors' championship.

The underperformer was Ricciardo, who failed to reach the podium and regularly lagged behind his teammate, although in Italy he achieved a meritorious redemption with a great victory at Monza, to finish eighth in the drivers' standings with 115 points.

As a team, McLaren was unable to hold on to third place in the constructors' championship. In addition to being overtaken by Mercedes and Red Bull, Ferrari also showed a clear improvement over their disastrous previous year, snatching third place from them.

However, there were grounds for optimism. The team had just begun its transition to Mercedes engines and there was room for improvement in adapting to them.

---

[97] Futbolred.com

Perhaps the double at Monza, with Ricciardo first and Norris second, was not so unexpected, but the result of a steady progression that could bring McLaren back into contention with the big boys.

In 2022, the revolutionary change of regulations was implemented with the aim of reducing costs and equalizing the competition.

Through a budget limit, the big differences between teams were limited in order to achieve a more equal grid. In addition, the flat bottom was eliminated and the ground effect was recovered in order to facilitate overtaking to increase the spectacular nature of the competition.

This forced a "fresh start" and put McLaren in a complicated situation: could it continue its progress towards the top positions or would such a drastic change break its progressive improvement?

The new MCL36 was designed with a short and narrow nose in order to lose weight, one of the big problems of the new designs.

In turn, the front was designed with the aim of channeling as much air as possible to the ground and pontoons to take advantage of the new ground effect, as well as having a large diffuser to receive all that airflow.

As for the chassis, the new McLaren renounced a very pronounced lower channel, giving priority to the pontoons and lowering the center of gravity to get a wider engine cover that would allow better cooling.

The car used the Mercedes-AMG F1 M13 engine.

The new MCL36 was driven for another year by Daniel Ricciardo and Lando Norris.

98 Caranddriver.com

The season got off to a decent start with Lando Norris scoring in two of the first three races, and taking the podium at the fourth event in Emilia-Romagna. This meant starting as in the previous campaign, without the significant changes in the competition having noticeably affected the team, and there was hope for more podium finishes on a more frequent basis.

However, this did not happen. For the rest of the season, Norris had to settle for frequent points finishes, which he achieved in seventeen of the 22 races. With 122 points, Norris finished a disappointing seventh in the final drivers' standings, in a year in which the young Briton saw his chances of continuing to show his progress and his ability to challenge for anything in Formula 1 frustrated.

In Ricciardo's case, his performance was much lower than expected. He managed to score points in only seven Grand Prix, scoring 37 points and finishing 11th in the final drivers' standings, in a difficult year for him that confirmed his poor time at McLaren.

As a team, McLaren dropped to fifth position, being overtaken by Red Bull, Ferrari, Mercedes, and losing in his personal fight against Alpine, in a year in which the Mercedes-powered cars saw their performance diminished with the new regulations.

With only one podium during the year and a conformist fifth position in the constructors' world championship, McLaren saw a complicated future with a new regulation that limited their ability to implement new solutions.

ACKNOWLEDGMENTS

To all of you who encourage my love for motoring, which has been the germ of this work.

To all of you who enjoy Formula 1 and make this a shared passion.

To all those who have made me some notes or corrections (and will continue to do so) to create a more truthful and accurate title.

To all the graphic resources referred to throughout the book, for making this text more attractive.

To all of you who send me your opinions and make this book something collective.

Thank you very much.
Charles Sanz.

MORE BOOKS BY CHARLES SANZ

THE HISTORY OF FORMULA 1 TO THE RHYTHM OF FAST LAP

Formula 1 is the obsession to be **the fastest on the asphalt**. It is the passion for that split second that separates success from failure.

We enjoy its cutting-edge **technology**, seeking to polish that piece that allows you to start a few thousandths from the stopwatch; develop the most powerful engine to make the car fly on the track or control the wind to turn it into a few extra kilometers per hour through aerodynamics.

And of course, we enjoy the **battles on the track** at the limit between life and death, overtaking off the track at more than 300 km / h, pianos devoured to the extreme assuming the risk of an accident or off the track ...

But above all, Formula 1 is its history. Let's face it, there's no race we see without bringing back memories of the glorious past. You don't enjoy this sport so much without knowing its route, its history, the greatness that one day was and will continue to be and that comes back to our minds every time the engines roar. It would not be covered with that halo of heroism without those times in which those heroes through the control of time and speed became legends on the asphalt.

MORE BOOKS BY CHARLES SANZ

THE HISTORY OF FORMULA 1 TO THE RHYTHM OF FAST LAP

Formula 1 is the obsession to be **the fastest on the asphalt**. It is the passion for that split second that separates success from failure.

We enjoy its cutting-edge **technology**, seeking to polish that piece that allows you to start a few thousandths from the stopwatch; develop the most powerful engine to make the car fly on the track or control the wind to turn it into a few extra kilometers per hour through aerodynamics.

And of course, we enjoy the **battles on the track** at the limit between life and death, overtaking off the track at more than 300 km / h, pianos devoured to the extreme assuming the risk of an accident or off the track.

But above all, Formula 1 is its history. Let's face it, there's no race we see without bringing back memories of the glorious past. You don't enjoy this sport so much without knowing its route, its history, the greatness that one day was and will continue to be and that comes back to our minds every time the engines roar. It would not be covered with that halo of heroism without those times in which those heroes through the control of time and speed became legends on the asphalt.

MORE BOOKS BY CHARLES SANZ

THE HISTORY OF FERRARI IN THE FORMULA 1 TO THE RHYTHM OF FAST LAP

When Enzo Ferrari set out to create his own motorsport team, he did not give up until he succeeded and took it to absolute success. In the early years, it would not take long to achieve glory through Alberto Ascari and fighting with and against Fangio. In the early years of the championship, Ferrari always managed to be at the top of Formula 1 through drivers such as Mike Hawthorn, Phil Hill and John Surtees, becoming a team that was always a candidate for victory. Between 1964 and 1974, the rise of British brands complicated Ferrari's trajectory in a complicated period, but Niki Lauda would end up becoming the savior who would lead the Scuderia back to winning championships.

After a new dark period where the championships resisted despite having drivers with the talent of Nigel Mansell or Alain Prost, a hero came to the rescue of the Italian team to provide it with the best years of its history: Michael Schumacher. After the departure of the legendary German, only Kimi Räikkönen managed to extend the triumph of Scuderia Ferrari, despite having champions like Alonso or Vettel.

In these pages you will enjoy the history of the most legendary team in Formula 1 in the form of a simple walk through time and through the keys to its trajectory so that you can enjoy its magnificent past in a light-hearted way.

MORE BOOKS BY CHARLES SANZ

THE HISTORY OF RED BULL IN FORMULA 1 AT RHYTHM OF FAST LAP

Who could have guessed that an energy drink brand could come to reign supreme in Formula 1? Red Bull's beginnings were as a sponsor through Sauber. Thus, with its financial contribution to the Swiss team, Red Bull achieved the team's first podium through German Heinz-Harald Frentzen, in addition to adding the brand's name to the team that saw the debut of a future champion: Kimi Räikkönen.

However, Red Bull's racing ambitions went further than that. In 2005, it bought the Jaguar team to create its own team. Who would have thought that this risky maneuver could end in success? Then came the moments of glory: David Coulthard's first podium finish in Monaco, or Toro Rosso's first victory at Monza and Red Bull's first victory in China by a Sebastian Vettel who ended up being key to Red Bull's golden era.

But Red Bull is much more than Sebastian Vettel's glory days. This book shows the trajectory of Red Bull in Formula 1 in a simple, light and through its main keys so you can enjoy wonderful memories or learn the past of this great team.

MORE BOOKS BY CHARLES SANZ

THE HISTORY OF RENAULT IN FORMULA 1 AT RHYTHM OF FAST LAP

In these pages you will discover or remember the origins of Renault, a whole story of overcoming from the ridiculed "yellow kettle" with its frequent explosions of white smoke to the first victory of Jean-Pierre Jabouille and the consecration of the turbo in Formula 1.

You will enjoy the arrival at Renault of Alain Prost, one of the best drivers in history, and his impact on the development of the team. You will also walk through Renault's golden era as an engine supplier, in its perfect partnership with the Williams of legendary drivers such as Nigel Mansell, Damon Hill or Ayrton Senna, or the Benetton of Michael Schumacher.

You will enjoy the glory days of the constructor after the arrival of Fernando Alonso to the team and the best years of its history, as well as the subsequent decline and the nightmare of crashgate, the provoked accident of Nelson Piquet Jr. that shook the foundations of the team. Finally, you will return to the years of uncertainty in its alliance with Lotus, subsequent sale of the team and its new return with the aim of, progressively, trying to recover performance in a convulsive hybrid era with the goal of returning to its best times.

MORE BOOKS BY CHARLES SANZ

THE HISTORY OF WILLIAMS IN FORMULA 1 AT RHYTHM OF FAST LAP

The Williams team is undoubtedly one of the most legendary in Formula 1 due to its long and successful history, with humble beginnings followed by an exciting rise to glory, with its subsequent fall and collapse.

This generated wonderful stories to remember, with Alan Jones pushing the team to the top and Clay Regazzoni achieving the first victory, or Carlos Reutemann fighting with a whole Nelson Piquet who would later also end up being part of Williams. The magic of Williams would lead Rosberg to be an atypical champion, and to attract the attention of legends such as Alain Prost or Nigel Mansell, who would end up being seduced by one of the most sophisticated and technological single-seaters in the history of Formula 1, capable of beating the almighty McLaren.

Even one of the greatest legends of Formula 1, the Brazilian Ayrton Senna, showed his recurring desire to drive for Williams, and his name would be linked to the British team for eternity. Only a motor racing prodigy like Michael Schumacher seemed to be able to stop the hegemony of Williams, having to resort to the limits of sportsmanship to compete with drivers like Damon Hill or Jacques Villeneuve.

MORE BOOKS BY CHARLES SANZ

THE HISTORY OF LOTUS IN FORMULA 1 AT RHYTHM OF FAST LAP

Lotus is one of the most legendary constructors in Formula 1, and one of those that has revolutionized the competition throughout its history with innovations such as the use of ground effect, the one-piece chassis or the incorporation of active suspension.

The history of Lotus is that of a team that was born and grew in the late 50s to achieve glory through a legend like Jim Clark. It came to dominate Formula 1 in the 1970s with magnificent drivers such as Graham Hill, Jochen Rindt and Emerson Fittipaldi. By taking advantage of the ground effect of the Lotus 78, the competition surrendered to the ingenuity of a team that led Andretti to become champion.

After its best period, Lotus continued to fight to win championships again, counting on future legends such as Nigel Mansell or Ayrton Senna. However, the legendary team had to face a progressive decline, and a difficult comeback in search of past glory.

MORE BOOKS BY CHARLES SANZ

THE PRIDE OF BEING FERRARI DRIVER – VOLUME 1

DO YOU KNOW THE HISTORY OF THE RIDERS WHO STARTED BUILDING THE FERRARI LEGEND IN FORMULA 1?

Scuderia Ferrari is undoubtedly one of the most legendary in the history of Formula 1. It is the team with the most championships won and the only one that has participated in all editions.

This means that all the drivers who managed to sit in a Scuderia Ferrari car ended up covered by a halo of heroism capable of transcending time. In this volume, we will take a walk through the stories of all the drivers who participated in the team during the 1950s: Ascari, the first great Ferrari legend; José Froilán González and the first victory for the Scuderia; Giuseppe Farina, the first F1 champion; Hawthorn and Collins' friendship to the detriment of Musso; Peter Collins and his enormous chivalry; Fangio and his talent beyond the mark...

MORE BOOKS BY CHARLES SANZ

THE HISTORY OF WORLD MOTORCYCLE CHAMPIONSHIP TO THE RHYTHM OF FAST LAP

MotoGP is the obsession to be the fastest on the asphalt on two wheels. It is the passion of riding an elite motorcycle and being part of the machine, sticking to it on every straight and tumbling on every curve. But above all, the world motorcycle championship is its history. There is no career that does not take us back to its glorious past, its legendary battles and exciting races etched in memory. You don't enjoy this sport so much without knowing its route and its evolution.

The legend of Giacomo Agostini, the absolute dominance of MV Augusta, the American hegemony with Freddie Spencer, Eddie Lawson and Wayne Rainey, the legacy of Doohan, the era of Valentino Rossi, the reign of the Spanish pilots ...

That is the objective of this book: a simple walk through its history to remember or learn about its origins and the years that mythologized this sport, to feel the weight of its past, thus adding another dose of passion to the best motorcycling championship in the world.

Manufactured by Amazon.ca
Acheson, AB